SECRETS OF
PAPILLOTE
COOKING

PAPILLOTE

Culinary Creations
Graphics
And
Photographs
By
Chantal & Gil Pique

A PAPILLOTE BOOK

Published by G .P Publishing House.
12200 Riverside Drive, Suite 2
Valley Village, California 91607

First Published in Brazil 1993 - Sponsored by Group *Accor* Brazil

All rights reserved. No part of this publication may be reproduced, stored in a retrieval system or transmitted, in any form or by any means, electronic, mechanical, photocopying, recording or otherwise, without the prior written permission of the publisher.

LIBRARY OF CONGRESS CATALOG CARD NUMBER 93 - 91897
Chantal & Gil Pique
PAPILLOTE - SECRET OF PAPILLOTE COOKING © 1993
© 1993 Photography by Chantal Pique
TX 3 554 842 1993
ISBN 0-9633688-7-7
I. Title: PAPILLOTE "No Mess Gourmet Cooking" II Title: Secret of Papillote Cooking.

The author, publisher and The Papillote Company, are not responsible for and make no representations, warranties, recommendations, endorsements or promises of any kind, either express or implied, regarding the safety, testing, effectiveness, durability, function, manufacture, availability or prices of the recipes or products and other items appearing in this book.

PAPILLOTE - Secret of PAPILLOTE Cooking -
was prepared and produced by
The PAPILLOTE Company.
Valley Village, California 91607, U S A

Text, recipes, photographic and food styling, and book design by Chantal & Gil Pique.© 1993

The PAPILLOTE Company ®

Printed in Hong Kong. 10 9 8 7 6 5 4 3 2 1

No Mess Gourmet Cooking

en Papillote

Gil Pique was born in Paris, France. After graduating from chef school, he spent the next 30 years perfecting the art of French cuisine in his own restaurants. Now living in California with his wife, Chantal, Pique dedicates his time to the writing of cookbooks.

Papillote is one in a series of single-subject cookbooks.

PAPILLOTE PREFACE

We created this book for you to use quickly and easily. We know you will discover, as we have, cooking en Papillote will change the way you think about food. Use the recipes as they are presented or experiment with then to suit your tastes. To either case, be prepared for the taste of exciting, and delicious, healthful meals without the drudgery of cleaning pots and pans!

PAPILLOTE CONTENTS

INTRODUCTION	14
COOKING MEDIUMS	16
CONVERSION TABLE	18
SUPPLIES	19
LEGEND	20
COOKING HINTS	21
FOLDING TECHNIQUE	22

RECIPES

HORS D'ŒUVRES	24
FISH & SEAFOOD	40
MEAT & POULTRY	56
VEGETABLES	72
DESSERTS	88
GLOSSARY	104
INDEX	106

PAPILLOTE INTRODUCTION

What is Papillote?

The term Papillote describes a preparation cooked and served in a wrapping of parchment paper, aluminum foil, or a roasting bag. Cooking en Papillote is similar to the idea of pressure cooking, but doesn't require the use of pots and pans. Fish, meat, poultry and vegetables are completely enclosed in their special cooking packets, retaining natural flavors, and more important, precious vitamins and minerals. Vitamins are preserved because they are not cooked away and food tastes more natural.

For the health conscious, en Papillote cooking is a delight because it is low in calories and uses no added fat or grease. The Papillote recipes we've included in this book are of Continental French origin with an Asian flair. All of the dishes are easy to make.

PAPILLOTE INTRODUCTION

The Papillote can be prepared early in the day, refrigerated, then brought to room temperature just before being baked. The parchment paper, aluminum foil and roasting bag are all recyclable.
In short:
Papillote means
NO MESS GOURMET COOKING!

Throughout history, humans have attempted to capture the natural flavors of food by cooking in sealed, pressurized containers. Archaeologists have discovered 4th Century B.C clay pots for this purpose. And for centuries, Pacific Islanders have enclosed their food in large banana leaves, recycling the leaves for fuel afterward.
The use of parchment paper as an enclosure was developed and refined in France. Whether using parchment paper, aluminum foil or a roasting bag, Papillote cooking preserves the health benefits of pressure cooking, but avoids both calories and heavy cleanup.

PAPILLOTE COOKING MEDIUMS

There are many variations in cooking en Papillote. For the recipes we've included here, three main cooking mediums are used: Parchment Paper, Aluminum Foil and Roasting Bag.
You may choose whichever medium suits you. They are interchangeable.

Parchment Paper

Parchment paper is an ancient method still used today for Papillote cooking. Able to withstand high oven temperatures, parchment paper retains heat, keeping a dish very warm for an extended period of time, protecting the flavor of the food. Easy to fold, the Papillote can be kept tight with staples.

PAPILLOTE COOKING MEDIUMS

Aluminum Foil

The versatility of heavy duty aluminum foil makes it well suited for Papillote cooking. Though not as elegant as parchment paper, it can keep a dish very warm for a long time. A neutral wrapping, like the parchment paper and roasting bag, it has no effect on the look or texture of the food. It can be used in direct contact with flame.
It is the only wrapping that can be used on the barbecue !

Roasting Bag

The roasting bag is made of transparent, seamless plastic film. It is absolutely odorless and taste free. One roasting bag allows you to cook for as many as six people.

PAPILLOTE CONVERSION TABLE

ALWAYS PRE-HEAT OVEN!

Oven Temperatures:
The following are approximate temperatures, rather than exact conversions:

Description	Degrees Fahrenheit	Degrees Celsius
Very cool	225	110
	250	120
Cool	275	140
	300	150
Moderate	325	160
	350	180
Moderately hot	375	190
	400	200
Hot	425	220
	450	230
Very hot	475	240

PAPILLOTE SUPPLIES

Some recipes will need supplies you may not normally use. These items are usually available in the International or Gourmet section of your local supermarket.

Parchment Paper
Roasting Bag
Chili Garlic Sauce
Rice Vinegar
Sesame Oil
Sesame Seeds
Soy Sauce
Sake
Wasabi
Extra Virgin Olive Oil

PAPILLOTE LEGEND

○	○ ○	○ ○ ○
very easy	easy	elaborate
$	$$	$$$
inexpensive	moderate	costly
-200 calories per serving	-300 calories per serving	+300 calories per serving
- : 15 TIME preparation cooking	- : 30 TIME preparation cooking	+ : 30 TIME preparation cooking

- ○ ○ easy
- $$$ costly
- - 200 calories
- - : 30 preparation
- - : 15 cooking

This simple visual system allows you to choose a recipe according to difficulty, cost, calories and time required.

4 servings

PAPILLOTE COOKING HINTS & REMINDERS

- *Use heavy duty aluminum foil.*
- *Always seal your Papillote completely.*
- *When using parchment paper or aluminum foil, check for punctures and leaks in your Papillote before cooking.*
- *Always use an ungreased baking sheet when cooking your Papillote.*
- *Depending on the size of the dish, add or subtract 5 minutes from the cooking time.*
- *When you open your cooked Papillote, be careful. The steam is very hot!*
- *Ovens may vary in temperature. Check your fish, poultry and meat by unsealing the Papillote. If more cooking time is needed, simply reseal and return the Papillote to your oven.*
- *Never use parchment paper or a roasting bag when cooking on a barbecue.*

PAPILLOTE - FOLDING TECHNIQUE - PARCHMENT PAPER

- *Cut a piece of parchment paper about 16 to 18 inches long.*
- *Spray with extra virgin olive oil.**
- *Place the ingredients in the middle of half the sheet and close.*
- *Starting at the front, make 1/2 inch folds. Repeat 4 or 5 times.*
- *Staples may be used to keep parchment in place.*

- *Now fold the open ends in the same way.*
- *Use staples to keep parchment in place.*
- *For best results, be sure to trap some air inside.*
- *Place the Papillote on a baking sheet before placing it in the oven. Leave enough room between each Papillote to let them inflate.*

- *After cooking is completed, serve each person an unopened Papillote or slit the Papillote open in the kitchen and slide the contents of each onto a dinner plate.*

 *If you do not have extra virgin olive oil spray, simply spread a thin layer of the oil instead. If you don't want to use any oil, that's fine, too!

PAPILLOTE - FOLDING TECHNIQUE - ALUMINUM FOIL

- *When using aluminum foil, follow the same folding pattern as with parchment paper.*

Staples will not be necessary.

Aluminum foil Papillote can be cooked in the oven or on a barbeque.

Technique for:
Cooking Rolled Food, Fish and Meat. Remember, the Papillote is great on the barbeque!
- *Cut a piece of foil about 16 to 18 inches long.*
- *Spray with extra virgin olive oil*.*
- *Place the ingredients in the middle of the sheet.*
- *Join the 2 ends at the top and fold down until foil encloses ingredients.*
- *Tightly twist each end to close your Papillote.*

- *To remove foil from cooked food rolls, you may first cut the covered rolls into one inch thick slices, then remove the foil*
- *After cooking is completed, serve each person an unopened Papillote or slit the Papillote open in the kitchen and slide the contents onto individual dinner plates.*

HORS D'OEUVRES

Spinach & Cheese Balls

Ham Rolls

Eggplant With Pepper Coulis

3 Pepper Shrimp

Stuffed Mushrooms With Crab Meat

Crab & Cucumber Rolls

Scallops In Tomato

SPINACH & CHEESE BALLS

INGREDIENTS:

- *4 bunches fresh leaf spinach, stalks removed, blanched, chopped and well drained*
- *4 thin slices of ham, chopped*
- *1 egg*
- *1 cup Swiss cheese, grated*
- *½ cup cottage cheese*
- *½ tsp. cumin*
- *1 pinch of nutmeg*

Sauce
- *½ cup lowfat yogurt*
- *2 tbsp. parmesan cheese*
- *2 tbsp. tomato paste*
  salt & pepper to taste

☐ In a bowl, thoroughly mix all ingredients (except sauce).
☐ Form balls into the size of a plum. You should have about 3 balls per serving.
☐ Cut four pieces of parchment paper or aluminum foil, or use one roasting bag.
☐ Arrange the balls in the middle.
☐ Tightly seal the Papillote and place it on a baking sheet.
☐ Bake for 10 minutes in 400° oven.

For the Sauce
☐ In an oven safe bowl, combine the yogurt, parmesan cheese, tomato paste, salt & pepper and mix well. Place in oven for 5 minutes.
☐ Pour sauce on plate and place balls on top.

| 4 servings | O very easy | $ inexpensive | - 300 calories | - : 15 preparation | - : 15 cooking |

HAM ROLLS

INGREDIENTS:

- *12 thin slices ham*
- *4 large mushrooms, finely diced*
- *4 tbsp. raisins*
- *1 cup feta cheese, crumbled*
- *2 tbsp. extra virgin olive oil*
- *4 tbsp. Swiss cheese, shredded*
- *4 green onions, finely sliced pepper, freshly ground*

☐ Dice 4 slices of ham.
☐ In a bowl mix mushrooms, feta cheese, green onions, diced ham and raisins.
☐ Add the extra virgin olive oil and freshly ground pepper.
☐ Place mixture at one end of each of the remaining ham slices.
☐ Firmly roll slices.
☐ Top the 8 rolls with the Swiss cheese.
☐ Cut four pieces of parchment paper or aluminum foil, or use one roasting bag.
☐ Arrange 2 rolls in the middle of each Papillote.
☐ Tightly seal the Papillote and place it on a baking sheet.
☐ Bake for 13 minutes in 425° oven.

| 4 servings | 0 very easy | $ inexpensive | - 300 calories | - : 15 preparation | - : 15 cooking |

EGGPLANT WITH PEPPER COULIS

INGREDIENTS:

- *2 eggplants*
- *¼ cup fresh basil, shredded*
- *1 large red onion, finely chopped*
- *4 cloves of garlic, pressed*
- *1 lemon, juice only*
- *4 tbsp. extra virgin olive oil*
- *1 tbsp. fresh thyme*

For The Coulis

- *2 red bell peppers*
- *2 yellow bell peppers*

For The Sauce

- *1 cup lowfat yogurt*
  salt & pepper to taste

☐ To make the coulis, broil the whole peppers in the oven, on a baking sheet, turning occasionally. When dark spots appear on the skin (about 7 minutes), remove the peppers from oven.
☐ Cover peppers with a damp cloth for 5 - 6 minutes.
☐ Remove the skin, cut peppers in half, take out the core and seeds. Cut the flesh into fine strips.
☐ In the food processor, make a puree of the yellow pepper, 1/2 cup yogurt, salt & pepper to taste. Refrigerate mixture until time to serve. Repeat for red pepper.
☐ Wash the eggplant. Trim the ends and save. Cut into 1/4 inch slices. Sprinkle salt over the flesh and leave for 10 minutes.
☐ Rinse salt off eggplant and pat dry.
☐ Meanwhile, peel and chop the ends of the eggplant.
☐ In a bowl, mix chopped eggplant ends, red onion, extra virgin olive oil, garlic, thyme, basil, lemon juice, salt & pepper.
☐ Place mixture between 2 slices of eggplant. Repeat until all ingredients are used.
☐ Cut four pieces of parchment paper or aluminum foil, or use one roasting bag.
☐ Arrange the slices of eggplant in the middle of your Papillote.
☐ Tightly seal the Papillote and place it on a baking sheet.
☐ Bake for 60 minutes in 400° oven.
☐ Spread 1/2 the plate with yellow coulis and 1/2 plate with red coulis. Arrange the slices of eggplant on top.
☐ Serve at room temperature.

3 PEPPER SHRIMP

INGREDIENTS:

- 20 jumbo shrimp
- ¼ red bell pepper,
  cut into a fine julienne.
- ¼ green bell pepper,
  cut into a fine julienne
- ¼ yellow bell pepper,
  cut into a fine julienne
- 1 red onion, diced
- 4 green onions, finely chopped
- 2 tbsp. parsley, chopped
- 4 tbsp. extra virgin olive oil
- 4 tsp. balsamic vinegar
- 4 tsp. soy sauce
- 4 dashes cayenne pepper

☐ Leave the shells on the shrimp. Slit the front of each shrimp from head to tail, creating a "butterfly".
☐ Cut the peppers, discarding the core and seeds. Cut the flesh into a fine julienne.
☐ In a bowl, mix the peppers, red onion, green onion and parsley. Add the extra virgin olive oil, balsamic vinegar, soy sauce and cayenne pepper.
☐ Add the shrimp and mix thoroughly.
☐ Cut four pieces of parchment paper or aluminum foil, or use one roasting bag.
☐ Arrange the vegetable mixture in the middle and place the shrimp on top. Add the remaining liquid.
☐ Tightly seal the Papillote and place it on a baking sheet.
☐ Bake for 12 minutes in 425° oven.
☐ Before serving, sprinkle chopped parsley over each portion.

| 4 servings | ○○ easy | $$ moderate | +300 calories | -:30 preparation | -:15 cooking |

STUFFED MUSHROOMS WITH CRAB MEAT

INGREDIENTS:

- 12 large mushrooms
- 1 cup crab meat or imitation
- ¼ cup fresh basil, finely shredded
- ½ cup bread crumbs
- 2 green onions, finely sliced
- 2 cloves garlic, pressed
- 4 tbsp. extra virgin olive oil
- 4 tbsp. soy sauce
  salt and pepper to taste

☐ In a bowl, mix the bread crumbs, garlic, basil and extra virgin olive oil, salt & pepper to taste and put aside.
☐ In another bowl, mix the crab meat, green onions and soy sauce.
☐ Remove the stems from the mushrooms.
☐ Stuff the mushrooms with the crab mixture and cover with the bread crumb mix.
☐ Cut four pieces parchment paper or aluminum foil, or use one roasting bag.
☐ Arrange the stuffed mushrooms in the middle.
☐ Tightly seal the Papillote and place it on a baking sheet.
☐ Bake for 15 minutes in 400° oven.

CRAB & CUCUMBER ROLLS

INGREDIENTS.

- *2 large cucumbers*
- *1 cup crab meat or imitation*
- *½ red bell pepper*
- *½ yellow bell pepper*
- *1 bunch chives*
  salt

Sauce
- *4 tbsp. soy sauce*
- *1 tsp. wasabi*
- *1 tsp. sesame seeds*
  chives, chopped

☐ Cut the cucumbers lengthwise into long, paper-thin slices, using a vegetable peeler.
☐ Salt lightly, let sit for 10 minutes, rinse and pat dry.
☐ Peel the bell peppers with a peeling knife and cut into a fine julienne.
☐ Form a sheet of cucumber slices by laying slices side by side, lengthwise, overlapping the edges (you'll use about 1/2 cucumber for each roll).
☐ At one end, arrange a wide band of crab meat. Make thin lines of red and yellow bell pepper and chives.
☐ Holding the ingredients firmly in place with your fingers, roll completely.
☐ Repeat with the remaining ingredients to make another roll. Make 4 rolls.
☐ Wrap each roll in a sheet of foil and twist the ends. Place it on a baking sheet.
☐ Bake for 7 minutes in 400° oven.
☐ Cut the roll into 1 inch slices and remove the foil.
For The Sauce:
☐ In an small bowl, combine the soy sauce and wasabi. Top with sesame seeds and chopped chives. Serve the sauce with the rolls.

SCALLOPS IN TOMATO

INGREDIENTS:

- *4 tomatoes*
- *12 scallops, washed well*
- *½ cup pre-cooked couscous*
- *1 medium carrot, finely chopped*
- *½ red onion, finely chopped*
- *2 tbsp. chives, finely chopped*
- *1 lemon (juice only)*
- *2 tbsp. extra virgin olive oil*
- *2 tbsp. soy sauce*
- *4 dashes cayenne pepper*

- [ ] In a bowl, mix the couscous, lemon juice and extra virgin olive oil. Saturate the couscous with 1/2 cup boiling water.
- [ ] Cover the bowl, allowing the couscous to swell (about 10 minutes).
- [ ] With a fork, separate the grain and mix with the chives, carrot and red onions.
- [ ] In another bowl, combine the scallops, soy sauce and cayenne pepper. Mix well.
- [ ] Cut the top off each tomato and with a tablespoon, remove the flesh and seeds. Stuff tomato with couscous and place 3 scallops on top. Sprinkle with chives.
- [ ] Cut 4 pieces of parchment paper or aluminum foil, or use one roasting bag.
- [ ] Arrange the tomatoes in the middle.
- [ ] Tightly seal the Papillote and place it on a baking sheet.
- [ ] Bake for 13 minutes in 425° oven.

4 servings | very easy | $ inexpensive | - 300 calories | - :30 preparation | - :15 cooking

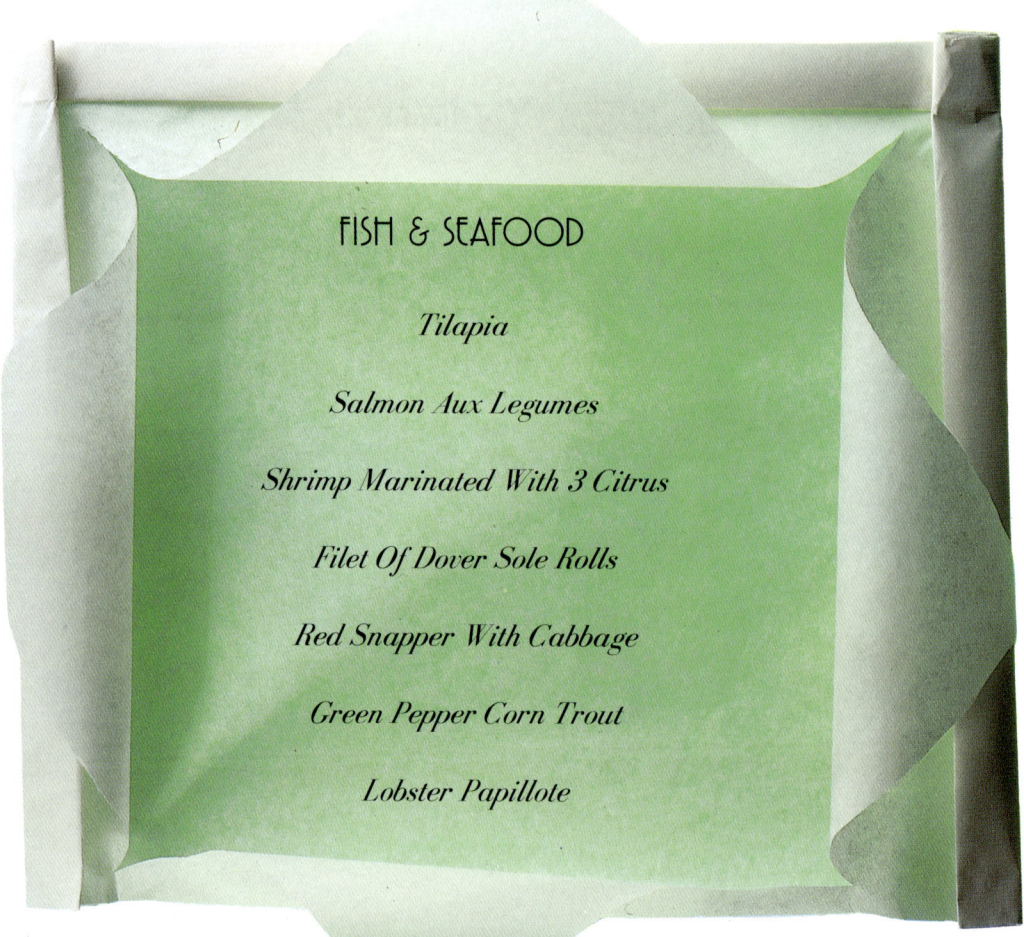

FISH & SEAFOOD

Tilapia

Salmon Aux Legumes

Shrimp Marinated With 3 Citrus

Filet Of Dover Sole Rolls

Red Snapper With Cabbage

Green Pepper Corn Trout

Lobster Papillote

TILAPIA

INGREDIENTS.

- *4 small tilapia, scaled and cleaned*
- *4 green onions, cut in fine julienne*
- *2 shallots, sliced*
- *1 green chili, finely diced*
- *1 tsp. fresh ginger, finely diced*
- *8 tbsp. soy sauce*
- *1 tbsp. wasabi*
- *4 tbsp. extra virgin olive oil*
- *1 tsp. sesame oil*

- ☐ Wash and pat dry the fish.
- ☐ With a sharp knife, make a shallow cross, about 1/4 inch deep, on the top of each side to allow the fish to absorb the flavor of the simmering liquid.
- ☐ In a bowl, combine ingredients and mix well. Add fish and marinate for 20 minutes in refrigerator.
- ☐ Cut four pieces of parchment paper or aluminum foil, or use one roasting bag.
- ☐ Arrange fish in the middle and place a tablespoon of marinade inside each fish.
- ☐ Pour the remaining marinade on top.
- ☐ Tightly seal the Papillote and place it on a baking sheet.
- ☐ Bake for 25 minutes in 425° oven.

SALMON AUX LEGUMES

INGREDIENTS.

- *1 filet of salmon, (about 1 lb.) cut into 4 pieces*
- *1 carrot, cut in fine julienne*
- *12 large mushrooms, finely sliced*
- *2 leeks (white only), finely sliced*
- *2 tbsp. soy sauce*
- *½ lemon, sliced*
- *½ lemon, cut peel into fine julienne*
- *½ cup fresh basil, finely shredded*
- *½ cup dry white wine*
- *4 dashes cayenne pepper salt & pepper to taste*

- ☐ In a bowl, mix carrots, leeks, mushrooms, lemon peel, lemon slices, basil, soy sauce and cayenne pepper.
- ☐ Cut four pieces of parchment paper or aluminum foil, or use one roasting bag.
- ☐ Arrange filet on top of vegetables and pour the wine over each portion.
- ☐ Tightly seal the Papillote and place it on a baking sheet.
- ☐ Bake for 20 minutes in 425° oven.

SHRIMP MARINATED WITH 3 CITRUS

INGREDIENTS:

- *20 large shrimp*
- *1 orange*
- *1 lemon*
- *1 lime*
- *2 tbsp. dill chopped*
- *2 tbsp. pink peppercorns*
- *4 tbsp. tequila*
  salt & pepper to taste

For The Sauce:

- *1 cup plain lowfat yogurt*
- *½ tsp. saffron*

☐ Shell and de-vein the shrimp, leaving the tails attached. Wash and pat dry.
☐ Peel the orange, lemon and lime with a peeling knife. Cut the skin into a fine julienne.
☐ Squeeze the juice from the fruit and set aside.
☐ Place the shrimp in a bowl. Add pink peppercorns, dill, the zest of the citrus (please see glossary), half of the juice, tequila, salt & pepper.
☐ Let marinate for 1 hour in refrigerator.
☐ Cut four pieces of parchment paper or aluminum foil, or use one roasting bag.
☐ Arrange the shrimp in the middle.
☐ Pour the marinade on top of the shrimp before closing the Papillotes.
☐ Tightly seal the Papillote and place it on a baking sheet.
☐ Bake for 10 minutes in 425° oven.
For The Sauce.
☐ In an oven-safe bowl, combine the yogurt, saffron and the rest of fruit juice. Salt & pepper to taste.
☐ Place in oven for 5 minutes.
☐ Serve with the shrimp.

- 4 servings
- ○ ○ easy
- $$ moderate
- + 300 calories
- + : 30 preparation
- - : 15 cooking

FILET OF DOVER SOLE ROLLS

INGREDIENTS.

- *12 small filets of Dover sole*
- *4 zucchini, cut into long strips*
- *¼ cup fresh parsley, finely chopped*
- *¼ cup raw almonds, sliced*
- *¼ cup capers*
- *1 lemon*
- *4 tbsp. of extra virgin olive oil*
- *1 tsp. of nutmeg*
  salt & pepper to taste

- ☐ Place filets on a plate. Peel 1/2 of lemon and cut peel into fine julienne. Squeeze lemon juice over filets. Salt & pepper to taste.
- ☐ Turn filets over. Repeat and set aside.
- ☐ In a bowl, combine parsley, almonds, capers, extra virgin olive oil, lemon peel and nutmeg. Mix well.
- ☐ Cut the zucchini into long strips using a vegetable peeler or a mandolin.
- ☐ Cover the filets with mixture. Roll each filet and wrap with a strip of zucchini. Use a toothpick to keep strip in place.
- ☐ Cut four pieces of parchment paper or aluminum foil, or use one roasting bag.
- ☐ Make a bed of zucchini strips. Arrange 3 rolls straight up in the middle.
- ☐ Pour the remaining juice over the rolls.
- ☐ Tightly seal the Papillote and place it on a baking sheet.
- ☐ Bake for 12 minutes in 425° oven.

4 servings | *○ ○ easy* | *$$ moderate* | *- 200 calories* | *- : 30 preparation* | *- : 15 cooking*

RED SNAPPER WITH CABBAGE

INGREDIENTS.

- *4 filets of red snapper (about 1 ¼ lbs.)*
- *1 savoy cabbage*
- *4 strips of bacon*
- *1 tbsp. pink peppercorn*
- *4 tbsp. soy sauce*
- *2 tbsp. extra virgin olive oil*

- [ ] Cut cabbage into julienne and blanch in boiling water for 2-3 minutes.
- [ ] Cut strips of bacon into julienne and blanch in boiling water for 2-3 minutes.
- [ ] In a bowl, combine cabbage, bacon, pink peppercorn, extra virgin olive oil and soy sauce.
- [ ] Cut four pieces of parchment paper or aluminum foil, or use one roasting bag.
- [ ] Arrange the filet in the middle and cover with mixture.
- [ ] Tightly seal the Papillote and place it on a baking sheet.
- [ ] Bake for 15 minutes in 425° oven.

4 servings	O very easy	$$ moderate	-200 calories	-:15 preparation	-:30 cooking

GREEN PEPPER CORN TROUT

INGREDIENTS.

- *4 small fresh trout, boneless*
- *2 tbsp. green peppercorns in brine*
- *4 tbsp. extra virgin olive oil*
- *2 cloves garlic, finely sliced*
- *1 lemon*
- *1 tbsp. fresh rosemary*
- *1 tbsp. fresh thyme*
- *2 tbsp. soy sauce*
  pepper to taste

☐ Peel 1/2 of lemon and cut peel into fine a julienne. In a bowl, mix lemon peel, lemon juice, green peppercorns, extra virgin olive oil, garlic, rosemary, thyme, soy sauce and pepper.
☐ Wash trout thoroughly and pat dry.
☐ Cut four pieces of parchment paper or aluminum foil, or use one roasting bag.
☐ Place trout in the middle. Inside each trout, place 1 teaspoon of mixture, pouring the remainder on top of the fish.
☐ Tightly seal the Papillote and place it on a baking sheet.
☐ Bake for 20 minutes in 425° oven.

| 4 servings | Ò very easy | $ inexpensive | - 300 calories | - : 15 preparation | - : 30 cooking |

LOBSTER PAPILLOTE

INGREDIENTS:

- *4 live lobsters (about 1 lb. each)*
- *4 green onions, finely sliced*
- *4 tbsp. Sczechuan spicy sauce*
- *4 tbsp. extra virgin olive oil*
- *2 tsp. chili garlic sauce*
- *2 tsp. sesame oil*

☐ Plunge the live lobsters into boiling water for 3 minutes.
☐ Remove the lobsters from water and let cool until easily handled.
☐ Split the lobster lengthwise through the undershell and flesh. Remove and discard the stomach sac and pull out the dark intestinal vein.
☐ In a bowl, set aside the creamy part (brine). Crack the claws.
☐ Remove the lobster meat from the shells and slice it.
☐ In a bowl, combine green onion, Sczechuan spicy sauce, chili garlic sauce, sesame oil, extra virgin olive oil and the creamy part from the lobster.
☐ Add the lobster meat and mix thoroughly.
☐ Place mixture in lobster shells.
☐ Cut four pieces of parchment paper or aluminum foil, or use one roasting bag.
☐ Arrange lobster in the middle.
☐ Tightly seal the Papillote and place it on a baking sheet.
☐ Bake for 13 minutes in 425° oven.

4 servings	○ ○ easy	$$$ costly	- 300 calories	- :30 preparation	- :15 cooking

MEAT & POULTRY

Veal Rolls

Chicken Drumsticks

Filet Mignon

Quail With Shiitake Mushroom

Double Papillote Chicken

Leg Of Lamb With Lemon

Cornish Game With Couscous

VEAL ROLLS

INGREDIENTS:

- *4 veal roundsteaks, cut into ½ inch slices*
- *8 thin slices prosciutto.*
- *12 small asparagus*
- *4 tbsp. parmesan cheese*
- *2 tbsp. cornstarch*
  salt & pepper to taste
  cooking string

- ☐ Trim the asparagus. Parboil in lightly salted water until tender.
- ☐ Trim veal and place it between sheets of parchment paper. Pound until flat. Handle flattened meat gently!
- ☐ Top each piece of veal with slices of prosciutto.
- ☐ Brush with cornstarch.
- ☐ Sprinkle with parmesan cheese.
- ☐ Lay 4 asparagus at one end of the veal strip. Roll firmly.
- ☐ Tie securely with cooking string. Repeat the process with the remaining veal, prosciutto and asparagus.
- ☐ Cut four pieces of parchment paper or aluminum foil, or use one roasting bag.
- ☐ Arrange the rolls in the middle.
- ☐ Tightly seal the Papillote and place it on a baking sheet.
- ☐ Bake for 20 minutes in 400° oven.
- ☐ Before serving, remove the string and cut the rolls into 1 inch thick slices.

| 4 servings | ○ ○ easy | $$ moderate | - 200 calories | - : 15 preparation | - : 30 cooking | 58 / 59 page |

CHICKEN DRUMSTICKS

INGREDIENTS:

- *8 chicken drumsticks, skinned*
- *3 tbsp. soft honey*
- *5 tbsp. soy sauce*
- *2 tbsp. rice vinegar*
- *2 tbsp. extra virgin olive oil*
- *2 tsp. cornstarch*
- *2 cloves garlic*
- *2 tbsp. fresh thyme*
- *2 tbsp. fresh rosemary*
- *12 small red potatoes*
- *freshly ground pepper*

☐ Press the garlic into a large bowl. Add honey, soy sauce, extra virgin olive oil, rice vinegar, cornstarch, fresh thyme, rosemary, freshly ground pepper. Mix well.
☐ Add drumsticks. Let marinate for 10 minutes.
☐ Wash the red potatoes.
☐ Cut four pieces of parchment paper or aluminum foil, or use one roasting bag.
☐ Arrange drumsticks and marinade in the middle and add potatoes.
☐ Tightly seal the Papillote and place it on a baking sheet.
☐ Bake for 40 minutes in 400° oven.
☐ Hint: For crispier meat, it will be necessary to cut open the Papillote prior to the last 10 minutes of cooking time.

4 servings | O very easy | $ inexpensive | - 300 calories | - : 30 preparation | + : 30 cooking

FILET MIGNON

INGREDIENTS:

- *1 filet mignon (2 lb. trimmed)*
- *4 carrots, cut into halves*
- *2 leeks (white only),*
  cut into halves
- *2 small turnips, sliced*
- *4 small red potatoes,*
  cut into halves
- *1 cup instant beef bouillon*
- *2 twigs parsley*
- *1 twig fresh thyme*
- *2 bay leaves*
- *2 dashes cinnamon*
  salt & pepper to taste
  cooking string

- ☐ Wash and pat dry all the vegetables.
- ☐ Prepare the beef bouillon with hot water.
- ☐ Take a piece of cooking string and tie the parsley, thyme and bay leaves together, making a bouquet.
- ☐ Sprinkle salt & pepper to taste on the meat and vegetables.
- ☐ Use one roasting bag.
- ☐ Place the meat inside, arranging the vegetables all around.
- ☐ Pour the bouillon on top and add the bouquet.
- ☐ Tightly seal the Papillote and place it on a baking sheet.
- ☐ Bake in 400° oven.

Rare:	25 minutes
Medium rare:	30-35 minutes
Medium:	35-40 minutes
Well done:	60 minutes or more

- ☐ Let the meat stand for 10 minutes before slicing.
- ☐ Sprinkle cinnamon on top of slices.
- ☐ Suggested garnishes: rock salt, cornichon pickles and/or mustard.

(4 servings) (O very easy) ($$$ costly) (- 300 calories) (- : 15 preparation) (+ : 30 cooking) (62 / 63 page)

QUAIL WITH SHIITAKE MUSHROOMS

INGREDIENTS:

- *8 quail, boneless*
- *8 oz shiitake mushrooms*
- *4 green onions, finely sliced*
- *1 lemon, juice only*
- *4 tbsp. soy sauce*
- *4 tbsp. Szechwan spicy sauce*
- *1 tbsp. sesame oil*

- ☐ In a bowl, mix the Szechwan spicy sauce with the lemon juice.
- ☐ Add quail and let marinate for 10 minutes.
- ☐ In a bowl, mix the shiitake mushrooms, green onions, soy sauce and sesame oil.
- ☐ Stuff the quail with the shiitake mushroom mixture.
- ☐ Cut four pieces of parchment paper or aluminum foil, or use one roasting bag.
- ☐ Arrange the quail in the middle. Add remaining sauce.
- ☐ Tightly seal the Papillote and place it on a baking sheet.
- ☐ Bake for 40 minutes in 400° oven.
- ☐ Hint: For crispier meat, it will be necessary to cut open the Papillote prior to the last 10 minutes of cooking time.

| 4 servings | 0 very easy | $$$ costly | - 300 calories | - : 30 preparation | + : 30 cooking |

DOUBLE PAPILLOTE CHICKEN

INGREDIENTS:

- *1 whole chicken (about 2 lb.)*
- *½ cup walnuts, finely chopped*
- *¼ cup fresh parsley, finely chopped*
- *¼ cup fresh basil, finely chopped*
- *2 tbsp. parmesan cheese, grated*
- *2 tbsp. Swiss cheese, grated*
- *1 egg*
- *¼ cup bread crumbs*
- *½ lemon peel, cut into fine julienne*
- *4 tbsp. extra virgin olive oil. salt & pepper to taste*

- ☐ Wash chicken thoroughly and pat dry.
- ☐ Starting at the neck, gently slide your fingertips between the skin and the meat to make room for the stuffing.
- ☐ In a bowl, mix the parsley, basil, walnuts, parmesan, Swiss cheese, egg, bread crumbs, lemon peel, 3 tbsp. extra virgin olive oil, salt & pepper to taste.
- ☐ Slide stuffing under skin. Going from the leg to the breast, use all of the stuffing.
- ☐ Cover the chicken with the rest of the extra virgin olive oil. Salt & pepper to taste.
- ☐ Use one roasting bag.
- ☐ Arrange the chicken inside.
- ☐ Tightly seal the Papillote and place it on a baking sheet.
- ☐ Bake for 60 minutes in 400° oven.
- ☐ Hint: For crispier meat, it will be necessary to cut open the Papillote prior to the last 10 minutes of cooking time.
- ☐ Let stand for 10 minutes before serving.

4 serving | O very easy | $$ moderate | +300 calories | −:15 preparation | +:30 cooking

LEG OF LAMB WITH LEMON

INGREDIENTS:

- *1 leg of lamb (4 to 5 lb.)*
- *4 lemons*
- *2 heads garlic*
- *1 tbsp. extra virgin olive oil*
- *½ bush parsley, stems removed*
- *1 tbsp. fresh thyme*
- *1 twig rosemary*
- *½ cup water*
  salt & pepper

- ☐ Cut 3 lemons into fine slices. Peel the skin of the last lemon and cut into a fine julienne. Press the juice and set aside.
- ☐ Cut one garlic head into fine slices.
- ☐ Divide the remaining garlic into individual cloves.
- ☐ Trim the leg of lamb. Place it on your working surface, skin side up.
- ☐ Make multiple punctures in the meat about 3 inches apart and 1 1/2 inches deep.
- ☐ Into the cut, slide 1 slice of lemon, 1 slice of garlic, parsley, thyme, rosemary, salt & pepper to taste.
- ☐ Use one roasting bag. Arrange the leg inside.
- ☐ In a bowl, mix the lemon juice, extra virgin olive oil and water.
- ☐ Pour the mixture and cloves of garlic into the roasting bag.
- ☐ Tightly seal the roasting bag and place it on a baking sheet.
- ☐ Bake for 75 minutes in 375° oven.
- ☐ Hint: For crispier meat, it will be necessary to cut open the Papillote prior to the last 10 minutes of cooking time.
- ☐ Allow the meat to stand in Papillote for 10 minutes.
- ☐ Remove lamb from Papillote. Thoroughly stir meat juice. Serve with garlic cloves and juice.

| 4 servings | ○ ○ easy | $$ moderate | - 300 calories | - : 30 preparation | + : 30 cooking |

CORNISH GAME HENS WITH COUSCOUS

INGREDIENTS:

- *2 Cornish game hens*
- *1 cup couscous, precooked*
- *1 red onion, finely diced*
- *1 carrot, finely diced*
- *4 tbsp. chives, finely chopped*
- *1 lemon (juice only)*
- *2 green onions, finely sliced*
- *4 tbsp. Szechwan spicy sauce.*
- *2 tbsp. extra virgin olive oil*
- *1 cup boiling water*
  salt & pepper to taste

- [ ] Cut Cornish game hen in half and remove the back bones.
- [ ] Loosen the skin from the breast and leg by gently sliding your fingertips between the skin and meat.
- [ ] In a bowl, combine green onions and Szechwan spicy sauce. Place hens in bowl and marinate for 15 minutes.
- [ ] In a bowl, mix the couscous, lemon juice, extra virgin olive oil, salt & pepper.
- [ ] Saturate the couscous with boiling water.
- [ ] Cover bowl with lid and allow couscous to swell (about 10 minutes).
- [ ] With a fork, separate the grain and mix with red onions, carrots and chives.
- [ ] Insert the couscous mixture under the skin, evenly covering the meat. Replace the skin and reshape the hens.
- [ ] Cut four pieces of parchment paper or aluminum foil, or use one roasting bag.
- [ ] Arrange the hens in the middle . Add the remaining marinade.
- [ ] Tightly seal the Papillote and place it on a baking sheet.
- [ ] Bake for 40 minutes in 400° oven.
- [ ] Hint: For crispier meat, it will be necessary to cut open the Papillote prior to the last 10 minutes of cooking time.

| 4 servings | ○ ○ easy | $ inexpensive | + 300 calories | - : 30 preparation | + : 30 cooking | 70 / 71 page |

VEGETABLES

Diced Potatoes

Spinach Salad

Asian Ratatouille

Leek & Green Onion Bundles

Vegetables Middle East

Stuffed Japanese Eggplant With Tofu

Belgian Endive Salad

DICED POTATOES

INGREDIENTS:

- *4 large potatoes, diced*
- *4 green onions, cut diagonally*
- *1 red onion, cut into thin slices.*
- *4 tsp. garlic sauce*
- *2 tbsp. soy sauce*
- *4 tbsp. extra virgin olive oil*
  freshly ground black pepper

- ☐ In a large bowl, combine potatoes with all other ingredients until well mixed.
- ☐ Cut four pieces of parchment paper or aluminum foil, or use one roasting bag.
- ☐ Arrange the potatoes in the middle.
- ☐ Tightly seal the Papillote and place it on a baking sheet.
- ☐ Bake for 30-35 minutes in 425° oven.

4 servings	○ very easy	$ inexpensive	- 200 calories	- : 15 preparation	+ : 30 cooking

SPINACH SALAD

INGREDIENTS:

- 2 bunches of spinach leaves, thick stalks removed and cleaned
- 2 cups bean sprouts
- 4 large mushrooms, cut into thin slices
- 4 large shallots, cut into thin slices
- 1 red bell pepper, cut into fine julienne
- 4 tbsp. extra virgin olive oil
- 2 tbsp. soy sauce
- 2 tsp. sesame oil
  freshly ground black pepper

☐ In a large bowl, combine all the ingredients until well mixed.
☐ Cut four pieces of parchment paper or aluminum foil, or use one roasting bag.
☐ Arrange the salad in the middle.
☐ Tightly seal the Papillote and place it on a baking sheet.
☐ Bake for 10 minutes in 400° oven.

| 4 servings |  very easy | $ inexpensive | - 200 calories | - : 15 preparation | - : 15 cooking |

ASIAN RATATOUILLE

INGREDIENTS:

- *2 Japanese eggplant*
- *2 medium zucchini*
- *2 medium yellow squash*
- *1 daikon*
- *8 cherry tomatoes*
- *4 tbsp. extra virgin olive oil*
- *4 tbsp. soy sauce*
- *2 cloves of garlic, pressed freshly ground pepper*

- [ ] Cut the Japanese eggplant, zucchini and squash into 1/4 inch slices.
- [ ] Cut the daikon into 1/4 inch squares.
- [ ] Cut the cherry tomatoes into halves.
- [ ] In a large bowl, combine all the ingredients until well mixed.
- [ ] Cut four pieces of parchment paper or aluminum foil, or use one roasting bag.
- [ ] Arrange mixture in the middle.
- [ ] Tightly seal the Papillote and place it on a baking sheet.
- [ ] Bake for 20 minutes in 425° oven.
- [ ] May be served at room temperature.

4 servings | O very easy | $ inexpensive | - 200 calories | - : 15 preparation | - : 30 cooking

LEEK & GREEN ONION BUNDLES

INGREDIENTS:

- *4 leeks (white section only)*
- *12 green onions*
- *4 tbsp extra virgin olive oil*
  salt & pepper to taste

☐ Wash the leeks thoroughly. Cut only the white section into a fine julienne about 3 inches long.
☐ With the green part of the leeks, make 12 long strips. These will serve as "ties" for the green onions. Blanch the strips in boiling water for a few minutes.
☐ Wash the green onions and cut them into fine julienne strips about 3 inches long.
☐ Save 12 long strips of green onion to use as "ties" for the leeks.
☐ Make 3 bundles per serving of leeks and tie them with the long green onion strips.
☐ Make 3 bundles per serving of green onions and tie them with the long leek strips.
☐ Cut four pieces of parchment paper or aluminum foil, or use one roasting bag.
☐ Arrange the tied bundles in the middle. Gently pour the extra virgin olive oil on top. Salt and pepper to taste.
☐ Tightly seal the Papillote and place it on a baking sheet.
☐ Bake for 25 minutes in 425° oven.

| 4 servings | ○ ○ easy | $ inexpensive | - 200 calories | - : 30 preparation | - : 30 cooking | 80 / 81 page |

VEGETABLES MIDDLE EAST

INGREDIENTS:

- *1 cup couscous, pre-cooked*
- *2 small potatoes, sliced*
- *1 Japanese eggplant, sliced*
- *4 medium tomatoes, sliced*
- *2 green chili peppers, finely diced*
- *4 cloves garlic, pressed*
- *4 tbsp. extra virgin olive oil*
- *1 tbsp. tomato paste*
- *1 cup instant beef bouillon*
- *1 tsp. paprika*
- *1 pinch cumin*
- *1 pinch coriander*
- *1 cup boiling water*
  salt & pepper to taste

☐ Place couscous in a bowl and add 1 cup boiling water.
☐ Place a lid on the bowl to allow couscous to swell (about 10 minutes).
☐ Prepare the beef bouillon. In a bowl, mix chili peppers, garlic, extra virgin olive oil, tomato paste, beef bouillon, paprika, cumin, coriander, salt & pepper.
☐ Cut four pieces of parchment paper or aluminum foil, or use one roasting bag.
☐ Arrange a circle of alternating tomato and eggplant slices.
☐ Spoon the couscous in the center of the circle and decorate with potato slices.
☐ Pour beef bouillon mixture on top.
☐ Tightly seal the Papillote and place it on a baking sheet.
☐ Bake for 60 minutes in 400° oven.

4 servings | 0 very easy | $ inexpensive | - 300 calories | - : 15 preparation | + : 30 cooking | 82 / 83 page

STUFFED JAPANESE EGGPLANT WITH TOFU

INGREDIENTS:

- *4 Japanese eggplant*
- *1 -10 oz package of tofu, cut into small cubes*
- *½ red bell pepper, cut into small cubes*
- *½ green bellpepper, cut into small cubes*
- *4 green onions, finely sliced*
- *2 tbsp. of soy sauce*
- *1 tbsp. fresh thyme*
- *1 tbsp. garlic sauce*
- *1 tbsp. extra virgin olive oil black pepper to taste*

- ☐ Wash the eggplant. About 1/3 from the top (see photo), cut lengthwise. With a tablespoon, remove flesh and cut into small cubes.
- ☐ In a bowl, mix all the ingredients. Add the eggplant and mix again.
- ☐ Stuff each eggplant with the mixture, forming a plump mound. Cover with the eggplant top.
- ☐ Cut four pieces of parchment paper or aluminum foil, or use one roasting bag.
- ☐ Arrange the eggplant in the middle.
- ☐ Tightly seal the Papillote and place it on a baking sheet.
- ☐ Bake for 25 minutes in 425° oven.

BELGIAN ENDIVE SALAD

INGREDIENTS:

- *4 Belgian endives, cut lengthwise into fine julienne.*
- *8 thin slices prosciutto, cut into thin strips*
- *1 tbsp. pink peppercorns*
- *1 tsp. granulated sugar*
- *2 tbsp. extra virgin olive oil salt and pepper to taste*

- [ ] In a large bowl, mix Belgian endives, prosciutto, pink peppercorns, sugar, extra virgin olive oil, salt and pepper to taste.
- [ ] Cut four pieces of parchment paper or aluminum foil, or use one roasting bag.
- [ ] Arrange the Belgian endive, strips of prosciutto and pink peppercorns in the middle.
- [ ] Tightly seal the Papillote and place it on a baking sheet.
- [ ] Bake for 7 minutes in 400° oven.

| 4 servings | 0 very easy | $$ moderate | -200 calories | -:15 preparation | -:30 cooking | 86/87 page |

DESSERTS

Delice of Bananas & Chocolate

Pineapple & Raisin Salad

Melting Pear

Apple Tart

Fresh Fruit Salad With Port

Pear & Pineapple Tart

Apricot Tart

DELICE OF BANANAS & CHOCOLATE

INGREDIENTS:

- *4 bananas*
- *2 oz. semi-sweet chocolate, grated*
- *2 oranges*
- *1 bunch fresh mint, leaves only*

☐ Cut four sheets of parchment paper. Place the grated chocolate on the bottom.
☐ Cut the bananas into 1 inch slices. Place on top of chocolate.
☐ Peel oranges with peeling knife and cut the skin into very fine julienne.
☐ Press the oranges and save the juice.
☐ Arrange the orange zest (please see glossary) and mint leaves on top of the bananas and pour the orange juice over fruit.
☐ Tightly seal the Papillote and place it on a baking sheet.
☐ Bake for 7 minutes in 400° oven.
☐ Serve warm.

---

4 servings | ○ very easy | $ inexpensive | - 200 calories | - : 15 preparation | - : 15 cooking

PINEAPPLE & RAISIN SALAD

INGREDIENTS:

- *1 small fresh pineapple*
- *4 tbsp. raisins*
- *½ cup white rum*
- *2 limes*
- *4 tbsp. brown sugar*

☐ Peel and quarter the pineapple, remove the center and dice the flesh.
☐ With a vegetable peeler, remove the skin of the lime and cut into a very fine julienne.
☐ Press lime juice into a bowl and add rum, raisin, sugar and lime peel.
☐ Let marinate for 10 minutes.
☐ Cut four pieces of parchment paper or aluminum foil, or use one roasting bag.
☐ Arrange the mixture in the middle.
☐ Tightly seal the Papillote and place it on a baking sheet.
☐ Bake for 10 minutes in 400° oven.
☐ Serve warm.

4 servings | ○ very easy | $ inexpensive | - 200 calories | - : 15 preparation | - : 15 cooking | 92 / 93 page

MELTING PEAR

INGREDIENTS:

- *4 pears*
- *4 tbsp. soft honey*
- *1 lemon, (juice only)*

- ☐ Peel the pears, cut into quarters and remove the cores. Slice quarters in half and rub each slice with lemon juice.
- ☐ Cut four pieces of parchment paper or aluminum foil, or use one roasting bag.
- ☐ Arrange 8 wedges in the center of the Papillote. Pour honey on top of pears.
- ☐ Tightly seal the Papillote and place it on a baking sheet.
- ☐ Bake for 10 minutes in 400° oven.
- ☐ Serve warm.

4 servings	Ò very easy	$ inexpensive	- 200 calories	- : 15 preparation	- : 15 cooking

APPLE TART

INGREDIENTS:

- *1 sheet frozen puff pastry*
- *4 apples*
- *4 tbsp. sugar*
- *⅓ cup flour*
- *1 egg, beaten with*
- *1 tsp. water*
   spray extra virgin olive oil
   cinnamon to taste

- ☐ Unfold pastry and place on lightly floured board. Roll into 14 x10-inches rectangle.
- ☐ Cut four one-inch strips from the long side, leaving a 10 X 10 inches square. Cut each strip in half.
- ☐ Divide the square into four squares, each 5 X 5 inches.
- ☐ Cut four sheets of parchment paper and spread with thin layer of extra virgin olive oil.
- ☐ Place pastry square on parchment paper.
- ☐ Prick dough several times with fork. Brush evenly with egg mixture.
- ☐ To create a "pastry bowl", arrange 4 dough strips along the outer edges of the square. These will be the sides of your bowl, so be sure the strips touch the bowl's bottom.
- ☐ Trim as necessary. Brush top strips with egg mixture.
- ☐ Repeat steps to form the remaining 3 pastry bowls.
- ☐ Sprinkle the pastry bottoms with sugar.
- ☐ Peel the apples, cut into halves and remove the cores.
- ☐ Cut one half of the apple into fine julienne and the other half into fine slices.
- ☐ Arrange the julienne strips on the bottom of each pastry bowl, then cover with the fine slices.
- ☐ Sprinkle with sugar and cinnamon.
- ☐ Tightly seal the Papillote and place it on a baking sheet.
- ☐ Bake for 45 minutes in 400° oven.

4 servings	○ ○ easy	$$ moderate	+ 300 calories	- :30 preparation	+ :30 cooking

FRESH FRUIT SALAD WITH PORT

INGREDIENTS:

- 4 fresh figs
- 1 peach
- 1 banana
- 1 bunch red grapes
- 1 bunch green grapes
- 2 plums
- 2 tbsp. brown sugar
- 4 tbsp. port
- 1 bunch fresh mint, (leaves only)

- [ ] Cut the banana into small slices and the figs into quarters. Remove the pits from the plum and peach.
- [ ] Cut fruit into wedges.
- [ ] Remove stems from grapes.
- [ ] In a bowl, mix sugar, port and mint. Add fruit and let marinate for 10 minutes.
- [ ] Cut four pieces of parchment paper or aluminum foil or use one roasting bag.
- [ ] Arrange fruit in the middle. Pour remaining liquid over fruit.
- [ ] Tightly seal the Papillote and place it on a baking sheet.
- [ ] Bake for 7 minutes in 400° oven.

| 4 servings |  very easy | $ inexpensive | - 200 calories | - : 15 preparation | - : 15 cooking | 98 / 99 page |

PEAR & PINEAPPLE TART

INGREDIENTS:

- 1 small fresh pineapple
- 2 pears
- 7 oz. pure almond paste
- 4 tbsp. almond slices
- 4 tbsp. chocolate chips
- 4 tbsp. chocolate fudge
- 4 tbsp. brown sugar
- 1 bunch fresh mint
  (leaves only)

- ☐ Peel the pineapple, cut into four 1/4-inch thick slices and remove the center.
- ☐ Cut four sheets of parchment paper and place one slice on each.
- ☐ Cover with brown sugar.
- ☐ Cut almond paste into paper thin slices and place on top of pineapple, covering slices completely.
- ☐ Arrange 6 - 7 mint leaves on top of the almond paste.
- ☐ Peel and cut the pears in half, core and cut into fine slices.
- ☐ Arrange pear slices on top of mint leaves. Garnish with chocolate chips and place a tablespoon of fudge on top. Finish with almond slices.
- ☐ Tightly seal the Papillote and place it on a baking sheet.
- ☐ Bake for 10 minutes in 400° oven.

| 4 servings |  easy | $$ moderate | - 300 calories | - : 30 preparation | - : 15 cooking | 100 / 101 page |

APRICOT TART

INGREDIENTS:

- *1 sheet frozen puff pastry*
- *12 large apricots.*
- *4 tbsp. granulated sugar*
- *4 tbsp. almonds, sliced*
- *1 egg, beaten with 1 tsp. water spray extra virgin olive oil*

- [ ] Unfold pastry and place on lightly floured board. Roll into 14 X 10 inches rectangle.
- [ ] Cut four one-inch strips from the long side, leaving a 10 X 10 inches square. Cut each strip in half.
- [ ] Divide the square into four smaller squares, each 5 X 5 inches.
- [ ] Cut four sheets of parchment paper and spread with a thin layer of olive oil.
- [ ] Place pastry square on parchment paper.
- [ ] Prick dough several times with fork. Brush evenly with egg mixture.
- [ ] To create a "pastry bowl", arrange 4 dough strips along the outer edges of the square. These will be the sides of your bowl, so be sure the strips touch the bowl's bottom.
- [ ] Trim as necessary. Brush top strips with egg mixture.
- [ ] Repeat steps to form the remaining 3 pastry bowls.
- [ ] Sprinkle the 4 pastry bottoms with sugar.
- [ ] Remove pits from apricots. Place 4 apricots, skin side up, into each bowl.
- [ ] Tightly seal the Papillote and place it on a baking sheet.
- [ ] Bake for 45 minutes in 400° oven.
- [ ] Let cool before removing from the Papillote.

- 4 servings
- ○ ○ easy
- $$ moderate
- + 300 calories
- - : 15 preparation
- + : 30 cooking

PAPILLOTES GLOSSARY

Blanching: Lightly pre-cooking raw ingredients for a short amount of time in boiling water. The ingredients are then refreshed in cold water and drained, or simply drained and then cooked normally.

Coulis: A liquid puré of cooked or uncooked vegetables or fruit.

Emincer: A French culinary term, it means to cut into thin slices. It is usually done to vegetables, fruit or meat with a slicing knife on a chopping board.
A mandolin (q.v.) or a food processor with a slicing disc may be used instead.

Julienne: Food, especially vegetables, cut into thin sticks. First cut with a sharp knife or a mandolin into even slices, $\frac{1}{4}$ inch thick or less, and then into strips two or more inches long.

PAPILLOTES GLOSSARY

Marinade: A seasoned liquid in which fish, meat, vegetables or fruit are steeped for varying lengths of time. Tenderizes and adds flavor.

Mandolin: A vegetable slicer consisting of two adjustable stainless steel blades held in a wooden or metal frame.

Parboiling: Please see blanching.

Tofu: A basic ingredient in Far Eastern cooking, especially Japanese. Tofu is originally from China. Derived from soy beans, it is relatively neutral in taste and rich in vegetable proteins.

Zest: The colored outer skin of an orange, lemon or other citrus fruit. The zest is separated from the whitish part of the skin by using a knife (called a zester) or a potato peeler. When cut into fine strips or small pieces, the zest (which can be blanched before cooking) adds flavor to the food.

PAPILLOTE INDEX

HORS D'OEUVRES

Crab & Cucumber Rolls	*36*
Eggplant With 2 Coulis	*30*
Ham Rolls	*28*
Scallop In Tomato	*38*
Spinach & Cheese Balls	*26*
Stuffed Mushroom With Crab Meat	*34*
3 Pepper Shrimp	*32*

FISH & SEAFOOD

Filet Of Dover Sole Roll	*48*
Green Pepper Corn Trout	*52*
Lobster Papillote	*54*
Red Snapper With Cabbage	*50*
Salmon Aux Legumes	*44*
Shrimp Marinated With 3 Citrus	*46*
Tilapia	*42*

MEAT & POULTRY

Chicken Drumstick	*60*
Cornish Game With Cous cous	*70*
Double Papillote Chicken	*66*
Filet Mignon	*62*
Leg of Lamb With Lemon	*68*
Quail With Shiitake Mushroom	*64*
Veal Rolls	*58*

PAPILLOTE INDEX

VEGETABLE

Asian Ratatouille	*78*
Belgian Endive Salad	*86*
Bundle of Leek & Green Onion	*80*
Diced Potatoes	*74*
Spinach Salad	*76*
Stuffed Japanese Eggplant With Tofu	*84*
Vegetable Middle East	*82*

DESSERT

Apple Tart	*96*
Apricot Tart	*102*
Delice of Bananas & Chocolate	*90*
Fresh Fruit Salad With Port	*98*
Melting Pear	*94*
Pear & Pineapple Tart	*100*
Pineapple & Raisin Salad	*92*

CONTENTS

Dessert	*88*
Fish & Seafood	*40*
Folding Techniques	*22*
Hors d' Œuvres	*24*
Legend	*20*
Meat & Poultry	*56*
Vegetables	*72*

ACKNOWLEDGEMENTS

We wish to express our gratitude to our daughter and son Mina and Jin Chang for their patience and help, our sister and brother-in-law Suzy and Jean Pierre Antherieu for supporting us in many ways, and our Minouche, for her love.
Special thanks to Firmin Antonio President of Ticket, Accor Brazil, for his trust and encouragement, and to Kent Snyder from Pier 1 Imports Northridge, California, for providing china and other accessories.

PAPILLOTE

OTHER G.P PUBLISHING HOUSE BOOKS
BY
CHANTAL & GIL PIQUE

Fish Dressed Up "En Papillote"

All About Chicken "En Papillote"

Vegetables "En Papillote"

Tofu For Every Day

Gourmet Salad

Your Favorite Desserts

Steam Cooking

Flower Arrangement